BRITAIN IN OLD PHOTOGRAPHS

TIPTON

JOHN BRIMBLE
AND KEITH HODGKINS

ALAN SUTTON PUBLISHING LIMITED

Alan Sutton Publishing Limited
Phoenix Mill · Far Thrupp · Stroud
Gloucestershire · GL5 2BU

First published 1995

Cover photographs: (front) The Fountain Inn, Owen Street, 1920s; (back) Victoria Park, *c.* 1925.

British Library Cataloguing in Publication Data.
A catalogue record for this book is available from the British Library.

ISBN 0-7509-0864-5

Typeset in 9/10 Sabon.
Typesetting and origination by
Alan Sutton Publishing Limited.
Printed in Great Britain by
Hartnolls, Bodmin, Cornwall.

For Tip'n folks everywhere

The Tipton Green Locks branch canal, *c.* 1960, flanked by the early nineteenth-century rows of houses named Lockside, Rifle Row and Horseshoe Row. The leaning chimney-stack belongs to Chatwin's Foundry and was a local landmark.

Contents

The coat of arms of the Borough of Tipton, granted with the Charter of Incorporation on 10 September 1938.

Introduction

The name Tipton evokes thoughts of a typical Black Country town, vibrant and industrial with narrow streets of tightly packed houses, factory chimneys belching out vast volumes of dense smoke, pit mounds and canals. This was the truth some years ago – indeed within living memory – but with the passing of the years and the processes of economic and political change there has been a transformation. Dense industry has been replaced by modern housing developments, green open spaces and trees. The black has in fact moved towards green. The transformation has been quite rapid and is an important reason for the production of this book. The older generation remembers the 'old Tipton' with deep affection and nostalgia but the younger generation has no conception of it. It is therefore important that a permanent record should be made for posterity.

Tipton has ancient origins – a Saxon settlement once existed here – but the modern town really began with the coming of the Industrial Revolution when the vast resources of coal, iron and clay beneath its surface were first exploited. Over the succeeding years the green fields and farms gave way to a sterile landscape of pit mounds, grime and smoke, and the face of Tipton continued to change with each new development. Now at a time of new economic change, Tipton is altering more radically than perhaps it has for nearly 200 years. Tiptonians are told that they are always looking to the past when they should be looking forward; maybe there is some truth in this, but while Tipton is not the prettiest place on earth its inhabitants have a fierce pride and passion for their town which is not easily understood by outsiders.

They are proud of its history for it can boast many achievements, the most notable of which is the production of the world's first iron steamship, the *Aaron Manby*. This vessel was constructed at the Horseley ironworks in 1822 and had trials on the Thames before spending many years plying the River Seine in France. The Horseley ironworks were also noted for the manufacture of iron bridges which were sent all over the world.

The Tipton 'Iron Master' Joseph Hall pioneered the puddling process of making iron at the Bloomfield ironworks in the 1830s, and this establishment became celebrated for a superior brand of iron known as BBH which was sought after worldwide. Dud Dudley, accredited with the discovery of smelting iron with coal in the early seventeenth century, had Tipton connections, and Sir Alfred Hickman who was to become known as the 'Iron King of the Midlands' was born here. Of the other prime industry, coal from Tipton helped in keeping Britain's wheels moving for many years, and as a tribute to its importance a huge lump of coal weighing some 6 tons from a Tipton colliery was displayed at the Great Exhibition of 1851.

Tipton gained its first canal in 1769 and the network grew to serve the expanding industries to such an extent that 13 miles of waterway ran within the parish boundary; this earned Tipton the epithet 'Venice of the Midlands' or, as it is known locally, 'Tip'n on the Cut'. The iron and coal industries declined in the late nineteenth century but Tipton showed resilience by attracting new engineering industries and maintained prosperity for many years to come. *Thunderbolt*, the car in which Captain Eyston broke the world land speed record with a speed of 357.5 mph in 1938, was made in Tipton in the year that the town was granted incorporation and became a municipal borough. So significant was this achievement that an armorial reference to the *Thunderbolt* was included on the coat of arms.

One industry to rise from the old was the manufacture of pumping equipment. The flooding of mines was from the early days of the Industrial Revolution recognized as a serious problem. Thomas Newcomen, the inventor of the atmospheric steam engine, erected an engine to pump water from mines near Coneygre in 1712. In the nineteenth century a levy was raised amongst the local mine owners and other industrialists to pay for a South Staffordshire Mines Drainage Commission in order to address this matter. The Tiptonian Edmund Howl, manager of the Drainage Commission, founded an engineering business to become known as Lee Howl & Co., which with foresight began to concentrate on the production of pumping equipment, eventually gaining a reputation as a world leader in this field.

The town is also proud of its sporting heroes. One of the most famous was William Perry, otherwise known as the 'Tipton Slasher', who became prize-fighting champion of England in 1850. The town has produced many talented footballers, while its Harriers club has produced many fine athletes, the most famous of all being the legendary marathon runner Jack Holden, who won fifty-seven major championships including the 1950 European and Commonwealth marathons.

Tipton has seen many changes in its history and has been able to surmount most of the problems it has faced, although the loss of its civic identity under the local government reorganization of 1966 was a severe blow to its pride. Passionate to maintain independence from their neighbours, Tiptonians formed a Civic Society in 1988; its members have helped in the preparation of this book which it is hoped will serve to encourage civic pride in the town and act as a permanent record of Tipton for old and new generations alike.

Section One

CIVIC LIFE

Members of the 1962–3 Tipton Borough Council, a photograph taken in the Council Chamber at the Municipal Buildings. Seated in the centre of the picture is the Mayor of Tipton, Councillor J. Walters, wearing his chain of office, and in front of him the large gilt mace. To the Mayor's right is the bewigged Town Clerk, Mr K.W. Madin, and at the far right of the picture, the Mace Bearer dressed in his livery.

The old Public Offices in Owen Street were built in 1876 and are pictured here in the 1930s. The site near the railway station is now occupied by a car park.

The Chairman of the Tipton Urban District Council, Councillor A.E. Bannister JP, laying the foundation stone of the Public Baths in April 1932.

James Edmond Salter, seen here with the scroll and casket presented to him on receiving the Freedom of the Borough of Tipton in 1963. A magistrate and Independent councillor for the Tibbington Ward, he was one of only two people to receive this honour; the other was Alderman A.E. Bolton, although sadly he died before receiving his honour. Councillor Salter also received the Freedom of West Bromwich in 1970.

Mrs Lucy Bagnall arriving at the Municipal Buildings in Sedgley Road West in 1936 to take her seat as councillor for the Horseley Heath Ward. The bouquet is presented by the young Miss Joyce Doughty (later Mrs J. Perks). Mrs Bagnall was the first woman to be elected to Tipton Council. Throughout the entire history of Tipton local government from 1855 to 1966 – the Local Board of Health, the Urban District Council and then the Borough Council – there were only seven women representatives.

The newly built Toll End Library in all its glory. It was designed by George W. Wenyon, the architect of the Central Library, and the memorial stone was laid in 1906 by Clarendon Hyde MP, the borough member. It was officially opened on 12 August 1907 by Councillor Joseph Powell, the then chairman of the Tipton Urban District Council. The library is an architectural gem amid the industrial surroundings of the Toll End area of Tipton.

The Municipal Buildings in Sedgley Road West, *c.* 1935. Built as the offices of Bean Industries Ltd, they were purchased by the council as the headquarters of Tipton's local government and opened on 7 March 1935 by the Rt Hon. Arthur Greenwood MP.

Mayoral Sunday, 1964, with the Mayor of Tipton, Councillor W.E. Drew JP, passing the Central Library in Victoria Road in procession on the way to church.

Councillor W.H. Powis JP, Chairman of the Tipton Urban District Council, meets HRH the Prince of Wales on the occasion of the official opening of the Birmingham–Wolverhampton New Road, 2 November 1927. Standing behind Councillor Powis is Councillor W.G.W. George.

Owen Street bedecked with flags and bunting to commemorate the visit to Tipton of Princes Marie Louise of Schleswig Holstein on 3 August 1909. The purpose of the royal visit was to enable the Princess to officially open a Nurses' Home in Lower Church Lane. The visit created much excitement amongst Tiptonians and celebrations took place throughout the day, culminating in a huge fireworks display on Victoria Park.

A parade passing along Ocker Hill Road, thought to be part of the celebrations for the visit of Princess Marie Louise in 1909.

Bunting and crowds in Dudley Road for the royal visit of Princess Marie Louise in 1909.

A reminder that before the local government reorganization of 1974 Tipton had always been part of Staffordshire. In the background is the sign of the Tipton Arms Hotel showing the coat of arms of the Borough of Tipton.

The official mayoral group photograph for Tipton's last year as an independent borough, 1965–6. From the left, Councillor Jonah Whitehouse (Mayor), his daughter Miss Joy Whitehouse (Mayoress), Mr J. Dutfield (Town Clerk), Mrs A. Lane (Deputy Mayoress) and Councillor W.T. Lane (Deputy Mayor).

Section Two

STREETSCAPES

Owen Street, February 1963. This central shopping area went into serious decline in the late 1960s and was comprehensively redeveloped ten years later, the Fountain Inn being one of the few buildings to survive.

Owen Street, 1930s. On the right is the Regent cinema which was formerly known as the Tivoli Music Hall.

Looking along Owen Street from near the railway station, *c.* 1910, showing the Albion Inn with its large lanterns suspended above the doorways.

The Tipton Co-operative Society Shop near the canal bridge in Owen Street, with its horse-drawn van standing outside, *c*. 1910.

Parkes's Commercial Academy, on the corner of Park Street and Victoria Road, early twentieth century. John Parkes was an expert in shorthand writing and taught his skills here.

Waterloo Street East pictured in 1969 shortly before demolition.

The junction of Sedgley Road East and Dudley Port. This had long been known as The Cross Keys, perpetuating the name of a public house that existed here in the nineteenth century. The photograph shows the junction as it looked in 1972 before the old buildings were demolished for redevelopment.

Brick Kiln Street, before slum clearance, 1930s. Visible on the right is the smithy of blacksmith Tom Brimble, whose trade was shoeing railway horses. The street took its name from an old field known as Brickiln Close.

Railway Street, 1970. The white building was constructed as a Methodist chapel in 1859 but was converted to the Victoria Palace cinema in 1912, a use it enjoyed until the mid-1950s.

Ocker Hill, *c.* 1910, showing The Crown and Cushion Inn of 1902 and the stately tower of the local Board School which was erected in 1899. The open-top tram is travelling from Dudley to Wednesbury via Princes End. The service was operated by steam trams from 1885 until electrification in 1907 but replaced by motor buses in 1930. There is a large thermometer attached to the façade of Gittin's shop.

Ocker Hill Road, *c.* 1920, with the chimney of the Birmingham Canal Navigation workshops rising above the rooftops. The attractive street lamp in the foreground is the same one as in the photograph above.

Back-to-back houses in Brewery Street, late 1960s, before their wholesale clearance.

Coppice Street in the mid-1930s, showing the concentration of early nineteenth-century dwellings which were about to be cleared. The section of cobbled street survived until the 1980s when it was salvaged by the Black Country Museum.

Great Bridge straddles the Tipton–West Bromwich parish boundary. This is a view from just beyond the boundary looking in the West Bromwich direction, *c.* 1900.

A view of Great Bridge looking towards New Road, *c.* 1900. Blackham the printer has a display of postcards in his window. Also seen here are the Union Supply Co. grocers, Farmer's the hatters and hosiers, while near the bridge is a clog manufacturer with a clog sign hanging outside his shop.

A scene in the Market Place, Great Bridge, around the turn of the century. The shops shown here include Ryder and Son, draper; Daniel Hipkins, butcher; Gavins, draper; and the coffee house run by Thomas Turner. On the extreme left is the Limerick Hotel.

Sheepwash Lane, with the austere looking Salem Chapel on the right, early 1960s.

Castle Road as it was in the early part of this century, soon after the houses were built. It was at that time a fashionable address.

Tividale Road, *c.* 1910. At that time the boundary between Tipton (on the left) and Dudley ran down the middle of the road but zigzagged further down to claim St Michael's Church for Tipton. The church was built in 1877–8 at a cost of £11,390.

Nos 6 and 7 Gilbert Street, Burnt Tree, shortly before demolition in 1972. With their high stone steps they were typical of hundreds of houses built in the early nineteenth century before the advent of building by-laws which laid down standards of design and construction.

Bell Street as it was in 1972 about three years before demolition. The Primitive Methodist Chapel can be seen in the lower half of the street in the distance. Bell Street took its name from the Bell Inn, which had disappeared long before this photograph was taken.

The corner of Bath Road and Anderson Road, 1970s. This was part of the Park Housing estate know locally as The Terraces: it was constructed in about 1900 at the same time that the nearby Victoria Park was laid out.

Confusion in Union Street after a bombing raid by Zeppelins, which appeared in the winter sky on 31 January 1916 and caused extensive damage to Union Street and Park Lane West. (See also p. 53.) The raid killed fourteen people and twenty-seven were taken to the Guest Hospital with injuries. For their parts in the rescue efforts after the raid, Mr Alfred North (later Mayor's Sergeant) and Mr A.G. Batten were both awarded OBEs.

Section Three

PRIDE IN THE JOB

Assembling the Thunderbolt *at Bean's factory, 1937. This car, driven by Capt. G. Eyston, went on to break the world speed record three times at Bonneville Flats, USA, culminating in 357.5 m.p.h. on 16 September 1938. It was symbolic that the Tipton Borough coat of arms which was granted with the Incorporation in 1938 should include a reference to a thunderbolt.*

A view inside Hale's Foundry, 1930s. Established in 1909 in Walsall, the company moved to Lower Church Lane, Tipton, in 1917.

A new colliery winding wheel is raised up on shear legs in the yard of W.M. Ward's Limerick Foundry, Great Bridge, *c.* 1880.

The Horseley works was noted for the manufacture of iron bridges which were sent to various parts of the world. The example shown here was a type supplied to the Chilean Railways in South America in 1910.

A group of workers at Buller's Foundry, Factory Road, *c.* 1910.

A workman displays examples from the range of large shackles produced by Joseph Wright at Neptune Forge, 1930s.

Workers cutting and boning meat for sausages and pies at Palethorpe's factory, *c.* 1910. Established in 1852 and operating in Tipton from this Dudley Port factory from 1890 to 1968, Palethorpe's claimed in its heyday to be the largest manufacturer of sausages in the world.

A 1920s pin-up girl advertises Palethorpe's products.

Palethorpe's Ltd displaying their range of English hams at the Dairy Show, 1904. The products gained three first prizes and three seconds.

Lathe's Foundry, *c.* 1920. The company specialized in the manufacture of iron ranges, fire grates and washing boilers.

Iron moulders await the next charge of molten metal from the furnace at Lathes Foundry, Summerhill, *c.* 1920.

Electrically welded ducts in the course of construction in No. 5 shop at W.G. Allen's factory, Princes End, 1947.

Girls assembling and packing grenades in Buller's factory during the First World War.

Hale's Foundry pattern shop, 1930s.

Horace Doughty in his uniform of messenger at the Tipton Post Office, 1920.

Humphries' dairy in Toll End Road, May Day 1941. The horse is decorated for the occasion. The Humphries family were the owners of Cotterill's Farm; here we see Jack Humphries with his young son David on the cart.

The joinery shop of the former Hope Works of Vono Ltd which stood in Dudley Port, *c.* 1930. In the 1950s the company claimed to be the largest single manufacturing unit of bedding and upholstery in the UK.

Section Four

BOOZERS

The Old King's Head public house, Dudley Road, 1968. Alongside ran Wades Passage, an alleyway named after William Wade, a grocer who arrived in Tipton from Lichfield in 1830.

The Fox Inn, Wednesbury Oak, around the turn of the century. The licensee at the time was Richard Caddick.

The sign of the flying swan denotes the White Swan public house at Burnt Tree, August 1968. The buildings on each side were demolished in the 1970s but the pub stood alone until its closure in 1983.

A Banks's brewery dray parked outside the Vine Inn, Gilbert Street, Burnt Tree, August 1968. The pub survived for another ten years.

The old Seven Stars, High Street, Princes End, *c.* 1922. The façade has advertising for Seedhouse's Pure Home Brewed Ales 3rd Prize and Diploma Brewers Exhibition, London. On the balcony it is noted that billiards and bowling were part of the recreation of the establishment.

The Fountain Inn, Owen Street, 1920s. Dating from the early nineteenth century, it was used as the headquarters of William Perry, the 'Tipton Slasher', prize-fighting champion of England from 1850 to 1857. The top storey was removed in the 1950s and the building was listed in 1982 in recognition of this historic association.

The Leopard Inn on the corner of Horseley Heath and Meeting Street. The photograph dates from 1970, five years before its demolition.

The Noah's Ark public house, Wood Street, 1968. The inaugural meeting of the Black Country Society was held there in 1967. The pub is best known for its association with the well-known local family of boxers, the Cartwrights.

The Black Cock public house on the corner of Owen Street and Union Street, 1968. The frosted glass windows depicted fighting cocks, a reminder that blood sports such as cock-fighting were popular in Tipton in the nineteenth century.

Originally the Round of Beef, this Owen Street pub was later renamed the Miners' Arms as a reminder of the past importance of coal mining in Tipton. The pub was closed in 1977 but lay empty for a decade before demolition.

The Prince of Wales public house at Princes End, 1934. Being on the north side of the main road the building was actually situated within the old Coseley Urban District boundary. The pub survived until 1979.

The Royal Oak, Dudley Port, 1910. The notice on one of the windows states that 'all tram cars stop here', obviously an inducement to travellers to have a drink whilst waiting for the next tram. The sign on the extreme right marks the entrance to the stables which were at the rear of the building.

The Black Horse, Park Lane West, pictured in July 1968 a couple of years before its demolition.

The Bridge Inn in Park Lane West, better known as Annie Harvey's after its long-time licensee, pictured with its adjoining houses in 1968. This distinctive local scene disappeared in 1972 and the site is now public open space.

The Nag's Head Inn, Groveland Road, *c.* 1935. The prominent sign above the doorway shows Alice Allsopp as the licensee with Ansell's beer well advertised.

The Victoria Inn on Dudley Road at its junction with Bell Street. The pub has long been known to the people of Tipton as The Bird, and is shown here in 1972 when still surrounded by houses. It was extensively renovated in the 1980s.

The Doughty Arms, November 1968. Named after Councillor W.W. Doughty, a past chairman of Tipton Urban District Council, the pub was taken over by the Little Pub Company in 1987 and renamed The Pie Factory.

Section Five

ON THE CUT

A view of the Great Bridge railway/canal interchange basin from Ryders Green bottom lock, April 1968. Ocker Hill power station is prominent in the background.

On 9 September 1899 the Birmingham canal was breached near Dudley Port when the bank collapsed into the marl hole of Rattlechain brick works. Such was the interest aroused that several postcard views of the scene were published, of which this is one.

A horse-drawn boat laden with slack from Sandwell Colliery to Ocker Hill Power Station passes the junction with the Haines Branch Canal in Great Bridge, having just descended the Ryders Green Locks, *c.* 1950.

Locals turn out to witness the unusual sight of a pleasure craft navigating Tipton Green Locks in 1957. By that date almost any boat was a rarity, as this section of canal was virtually disused, being officially abandoned in 1966.

The octagonal canal tollhouse and Tipton Green bridge, 1957. The tollhouse was dismantled in 1971 for eventual rebuilding on the then fledgling Black Country Museum.

A horse-drawn narrow boat glides along the Walsall canal past Ocker Hill power station, 1965.

Looking along Tipton Green Locks branch canal from Union Street with the top locks and Beehive Bridge in the distance. The canal was completed in 1801 but had fallen into disuse when this photograph was taken in 1960.

The coal wharf of Thomas Marsters Ltd off Bayleys Lane, Ocker Hill, 1965. The coal boats are being unloaded by hand. The wharf was situated at the end of the Lower Ocker Hill branch canal which has survived intact into the 1990s.

A pair of Willow Wren boats moored at the Tailby and Cox wharf on the Haines branch canal in Great Bridge in 1966, having just delivered a load of timber from Brentford.

The same pair, *Coleshill* and *Cygnus*, at the Tailby and Cox wharf, 1965. This timber traffic was some of the last commercial canal carrying into the Black Country from outside the region. When it ceased in late 1966 the Haines branch fell into disuse.

Union Street bridge on the Tipton Green Locks section in 1957, showing the turnover arrangement which allowed boat horses to cross from one side to the other without having to detach the towrope. On the right is the Tipton Conservative Club. The huge election poster on the wall urges electors to 'Vote for Frederick Cooper'.

The aftermath of the Zeppelin raid of January 1916, showing bomb damage to houses along the canal towpath of the Tipton Green Locks branch canal near Union Street bridge. In the background next to the bridge is the Globe Inn with an advert for Harper's Ales painted on the façade. Richard Andrew Harper also owned the Cottage Spring in Toll End.

In 1957 the iron aqueduct carrying the New main line canal over the South Staffordshire railway at Dudley Port was replaced by a concrete structure. The new bridge was constructed next to the old and moved across into place following the demolition of the original in order to minimize stoppage to the canal. On the right can be seen the new bridge ready to take up its position, while in the distance the 'Dudley Dodger' awaits connections in the island platform of Dudley Port high level station.

The huge brick structure of Ryland Aqueduct carried the Birmingham New Main Line canal across the road at Dudley Port from 1836 until its demolition, shown here in 1967. One of the pedestrians' pavement tunnels can still be seen. Beneath the new railway bridge is the bricked up arch which gave access to the canal towpath, known locally as the Devil's Hole. One of the aqueduct's large cast-iron name plates is preserved at the Waterways Museum at Stoke Bruerne, Northamptonshire.

An artist's impression of W. Barrows and Son's Bloomfield ironworks *c.* 1870, which graphically illustrates the importance of the canal system to Tipton's industries. The bridge on the left carries Bloomfield Road.

Replacement of lock gates in progress on the Toll End Communication Canal, 1950s. The lock is the second down from the New Main Line canal at Workhouse Bridge which carries Alexandra Road. Sadly this canal was abandoned in 1966 and has since been almost totally obliterated.

The Owen Street coal wharf of C.W. Mitchard, with 'best Cannock coals' being unloaded by the traditional method, 1957. Coal traffic was the staple trade of the Black Country canals right up to the end of commercial carrying.

The ornate cast ironwork of Factory Bridge designed by Thomas Telford and erected in 1825, pictured in 1969, a year before being moved for road widening. The old bridge was replaced by a new concrete structure and owing to the efforts of the Black Country Society the ironwork was saved and taken to the Black Country Museum.

An Alfred Matty motorboat entering the northern portal of the Netherton Tunnel, 1970. Although situated several hunded metres outside the Tipton Borough boundary, modern postcode divisions have put this section of the canal and tunnel mouth into the Tipton DY4 postal district.

Peace and tranquillity as swans glide on the Old Main Line canal at Princes End, 1952. The Summerhill Ironworks once stood close to here and its proprietors, the Millington family, were major benefactors to the Gospel Oak Methodist Church which can be seen in the background.

The kilns of the tile department of Lathe's Foundry reflect in the still waters of the Old Main Line canal at Summerhill, 1952.

The small cast-iron cantilever bridge at Factory Locks after a snow storm in February 1969; the houses of Furnace Parade are in the background. The locks and the small bridge are now listed buildings.

Section Six

SHOPS

The former Globe Inn, Union Street, in its converted state as a fish and chip shop, 1970.

Charles Cox's shop at the corner of Denbigh Road, Horseley Heath, *c.* 1890. An array of advertisements covers its façade; the notice on the window gives details of a house to let.

Smith's Port Stores in Horseley Heath, *c.* 1930. The well-stocked windows show that a wide range of goods was sold there.

The Tipton Co-operative Society store at Powis Avenue next to the gates of Jubilee Park, *c.* 1935. Norman Guest stands in the doorway.

A Stanton coach parked outside Sowry Boots Shop which stood next to their garage in Horseley Heath, *c.* 1950. The vehicle comprised of a Guy chassis with bodywork by Burlington of Blackpool. Stanton's began in 1906 with a horse and cart and brought their first coach (an AJS) in 1931. The coach part of their business was eventually sold to Kendrick's of Princes End in 1955.

The shop at 78 New Road, Great Bridge, owned by Charles Clee, 1921.

Ellis Billingham's shop in Sedgley Road West, *c.* 1909. In the pushchair is his son Alfred and behind is his wife Gertie. Ellis Billingham was a newsagent and tobacconist; the news placards outside the shop give a flavour of the time. Billingham senior was an amateur photographer and took many scenes in Tipton before the First World War.

A West Bromwich Corporation bus on the 268 route passing the market in front of the Limerick public house, Great Bridge, August 1968.

Great Bridge open market in 1968, showing the characterful but cramped and dangerous situation of its site, which led to its relocation to nearby Mill Street in the early 1970s.

Miss Baker's tea rooms on the corner of Union Street and Albion Street, 1930s. Earlier in the century the shop had been occupied by Mr and Mrs Joseph Whitehouse and it was here that their son Jonah, who was to become the last mayor of Tipton, was born in 1905.

Thomas Roberts stands in the doorway of his general hardware shop in Laburnum Road, 1938.

Shops in Owen Street decorated for the royal visit, 1909. The shop in the foreground is that of Harry Johnson, fruitier and poultry dealer.

One of Tipton's numerous fish and chip shops – Dickinson's at Horseley Heath, 1971.

Section Seven

SPORT AND LEISURE

The Tipton Harriers at the official opening of their Sedgley Road headquarters, June 1936. In the centre is club benefactor Henry Palethorpe, of the famous sausage firm. On his right is Jack Holden, the Harriers' most famous athlete.

The members of Binfield Street Jap Band congregated on Victoria Park, 1930. Beneath the banner is the leader, Richard Thomas, who worked as an iron moulder for Charles Lathe & Co.

Local pigeon flyers meet in the back yard of the Black Horse public house in Bloomfield Road, 1928. Note the stoneware beer mugs.

An early view of Victoria Park's main entrance. Created to commemorate Queen Victoria's Diamond Jubilee, the park was developed from derelict mining land and opened on 29 July 1901 by the Earl of Dartmouth amid great celebrations.

The inhabitants of Boscobel Street celebrating the end of the Second World War with a street party.

Collecting for the war effort at Tipton Green during the First World War. The display is carried by a horse and cart owned by J. Hartland of the Foxyards. Note the effigy of the Kaiser beneath the mock drop hammer.

Another picture of street collections at Tipton Green for the First World War effort, this time with a Buller's Foundry cart with an appropriate message.

Victoria Park, showing the boating lake, bandstand and war memorial, *c.* 1925.

The Tipton entrance to Dudley Castle grounds in the woods at Castle Mill, *c.* 1900. The lodge has long disappeared.

People standing around the unlit bonfire built on Cotterill's Farm fields to celebrate the Coronation of George V in 1911.

The ornate bandstand on Victoria Park, 1920s. It stood in a picturesque setting amid the green lawns above the park pool and was erected around the time that the park was officially opened in 1901. A favourite gathering place for Tiptonians on summer Sunday evenings to enjoy local brass bands, it was still in use into the 1950s, a band concert being held there on Coronation Day in 1953, but as other forms of entertainment evolved the band stand's use declined until it was demolished in the early 1960s.

Palethorpes FC during the 1953/4 season when they won the three trophies shown in the foreground. These were the St John's Ambulance Cup, the Lewis Cup and the Handsworth League Shield. The players are (back row, left to right) Millward (manager), Evans, Faulkener, Wagstaff, Cresswell, Barton; (front row, left to right) -?-, Kelsey, Dyke, Andrews, Mason and Halford.

The Conservative Club in Union Street, decorated with streamers and emblems to commemorate the Coronation of King George VI in 1937. The club building, dating from the early nineteenth century when it was used as a flour mill, is little altered from its original state, apart from the removal of a large window.

A women's outing from the Foxyards Inn (otherwise known as the Rag and Mop), 1920s. The publican Mr Groucutt stands proudly on the right, while third left in the coach is Georgina the Gypsy. She lived in a wigwam-type tent next to her father's caravan at the rear of the public house and was a colourful character who toured the local streets selling clothes pegs.

Stanton Brothers' coaches stand by in Horseley Road to take employees of the Horseley Bridge & Thomas Piggott Co. on a works outing in the early 1950s. Stanton coaches, which operated out of nearby Horseley Heath, began in 1906 with a horse and cart and bought their first coach (an AJS) in 1931. The coach part of the business was sold to Kendrick's of Princes End in 1955.

Hall Street decorated for the Coronation of George VI in 1936, with children enjoying the festivities.

Toll End Wesley Football Club, 1937–8. Toll End Wesley has long been a leading football club in Tipton. Thought to be have been formed in about 1903, the club's records date back to 1906 when the team played in the West Bromwich Chapel League. The club, which had its headquarters in the half-lit backwater of Wesley Place, hidden from the main road, had many successes and won numerous trophies including the coveted Dudley Guest Hospital Cup. Over the years many talented players have been associated with the club, some progressing to professional football, such as Ike Clarke and Malcolm Clews.

The main entrance of Victoria Park, 1930s. The ornate gates and gas lamps have since been removed but the posts still remain. The lodge was built by J. Gittings of Bloomfield Road and was demolished in the 1960s. The two large flower pots on either side of the drive were the gift of Councillor W.W. Doughty, one-time chairman of the Tipton Urban District Council. In the background on the opposite side of Victoria Road is the Holbeche Maternity Home, once the home of John Parkes, assistant parish overseer and author.

A 1950s scene in Victoria Park, showing the cenotaph and bandstand.

Princess Elizabeth meets Jack Holden of Tipton Harriers on 14 June 1949, following his victory in the annual Windsor to Chiswick marathon. Jack won this race on four consecutive occasions, from 1948 to 1951.

The Sons of Rest building in Victoria Road, shortly after it opened in 1961. The Central Library can be seen in the background, a quite spectacular Edwardian Freestyle building of red brick and yellow terracotta, designed by the Tipton architect George. H. Wenyon and opened in 1906.

Section Eight

TIP'N FOLKS

A group of people gathered around a gin pulley getting 'illegal' coal at the time of the 1926 General Strike. The man pulling the rope was named Griffiths; he lived in the Horseley Heath area.

A group of railway employees assemble on the steps outside Owen Street railway station in the 1920s, awaiting to board a train for their works outing.

Tom Langley signing copies at the launch of his book *The Tipton Slasher: His Life and Times*. The event took place in July 1969 at the Fountain Inn, Owen Street.

Joseph Hall (1789–1862), the 'Iron Master' who was a partner in the Bloomfield Ironworks which was founded in about 1829. Hall was regarded as the leading pioneer of the puddling process and, with his partner Barrows, made the ironworks at Bloomfield one of the leading establishments of its kind in the country, producing a highly regarded brand of iron known as BBH. He lived in Tipton for about sixty years but spent his last days at Edgbaston, Birmingham and was buried at Key Hill Cemetery. At the time of his death, Bloomfield ironworks was producing approximately 1,000 tons of iron a week and would continue to do so until the factory was closed in 1902.

Tipton St John's Ambulance Brigade, winners of the Maconochie Cup in 1918. Seen here are Acting Corporal J.L. Lyons, with Ptes Powell, Bennett, Stinson and Venables.

A group of youngsters in Horseley Heath, during the Tipton Carnival, July 1930. Encouraged by the grown ups they dressed up and held their own procession.

In June 1954 the old Regent cinema in Owen Street was reopened as the New Regal following refurbishment. The event was attended by the Summerhill Boys' Brigade and civic dignitaries including Councillor Jonah Whitehouse, to the left of the drum.

Workers from Chatwins Foundry, with their delivery van in the background, *c.* 1925. There were over sixty people employed here; the site is now occupied by the Chatwins Wharf housing development.

A Tipton family picking hops in the hop fields of Worcestershire, 1940s. Each year in about September hundreds of local families made a mass exodus to the countryside. For most this was the only holiday that they ever had but at least it gave them the opportunity to breathe fresh air.

Revd William Tighe Ker, the vicar of Tipton 1847–72. He was educated at Trinity College, Dublin and spent some time working for the church in Ireland and the east of England before becoming the incumbent at Tipton. He made himself aware of the social necessities of his new industrial place of residence and played no small part in the removal of existing nuisances. He was chairman of the Sanitary Committees set up in the parish between 1848 and 1853 to deal with the outbreaks of cholera, and in 1855 became the first chairman of the Tipton Local Board of Health. He was a fluent speaker and though of a somewhat eccentric nature he was held in respect by his fellow men and was esteemed for his kind-heartedness, genial wit and humour. A dedicated student of theology, during his time in Tipton he was the author of several works of a religious nature. When he died in Balham, London, aged ninety-two, he was one of the country's oldest clergymen.

A Buller's horse and cart collecting breeze and coke from Factory Basin, 1928.

A family gathering to celebrate a christening in 1907 at Holbeche, Victoria Road, the home of John Parkes (fourth from left, back row). Parkes was a journalist who in 1915 published his *History of Tipton*, the most important book ever written on the town. He was for a time editor of the *Tipton Herald* newspaper and was also an expert in shorthand writing. He taught this skill at various colleges including the one he founded himself in Tipton, Parkes Commercial Academy and Business Training College, which was housed at Holbeche.

A VE day tea party for the young being held in Doughty Street, Horseley Heath, 1945. In the background can be seen the Star Hotel (now the Port 'n' Ale).

George Bentley, a cornet player with the old Princes End Prize Band, *c.* 1920.

The opening of the Coppice Street Methodist Mission Christmas Bazaar in 1954 was carried out by the MP for Rowley Regis and Tipton, the Rt Hon. Arthur Henderson (second from the right). Looking on are (from left) Councillor Jonah Whitehouse, Revd A.J. Skyrme, Councillor Mrs Olive Gutteridge and Mr Parker.

Some of the town's larger industrial concerns had their own fire departments in case of emergencies. Shown here is the Vono Ltd fire brigade, *c.* 1950.

Corporal Joseph Davies, the only winner of the Victoria Cross to be born in Tipton. He was born on 28 April 1889 at Nock Street and educated at Great Bridge School. On leaving school he became a colliery-worker and later joined the Welsh Fusiliers. He won the VC on 20 July 1916 before an attack on the enemy at Delville Wood in France. Corp. Davies and eight men became separated from the rest of the camp when the enemy delivered a second counter-attack. Davies got his men into a shell hole and by throwing bombs and opening rapid fire routed the enemy. He then followed up by bayoneting several of the attackers. The citation spoke of his magnificent pluck and determination. He also won the Russian Order of St George (1st Class) for valour. He died at Bournemouth in 1976 and his medals were left to the Regimental Museum at Caernarfon Castle in Wales.

Christmas 1948 being celebrated in the English Oak, Upper Church Lane, by the staff of the railway goods station at Owen Street.

Tipton Post Office staff, *c*. 1900.

Section Nine

THE INDUSTRIAL LANDSCAPE

An engraving of Plant and Fisher's Dudley Port ironworks as they appeared in about 1860. The works are perpetuated by the name Fisher Street which still exists near to the site.

An aerial photograph of Tipton Green, 25 April 1955.

Willingsworth Furnaces, seen here in a postcard view of about 1900, were established in 1827 on the Gospel Oak branch canal. The site was developed as the Burberry Grange housing estate in the 1980s.

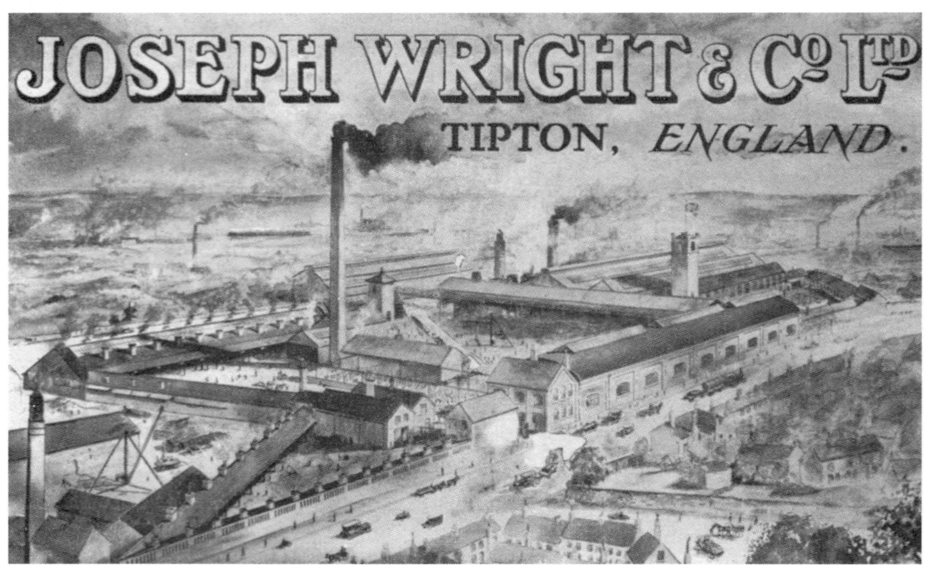

An artist's impression of the Neptune Works of Joseph Wright and Co., manufacturers of chains and anchors, taken from the 1937 company catalogue. In the foreground is Sedgley Road West.

The Patent Borax Soap factory, Albion Street, 1972. The buildings were demolished in 1979.

Looking across to the works of Horseley Bridge & Thomas Piggott Ltd from the GPO sorting office above the roofs of nineteenth-century buildings in Railway Street, 1961. The large white gable in the centre of the picture is that of the Durham Ox Inn.

Ocker Hill cooling towers viewed from the north, 1962. A diesel parcels' railcar waits for the signal to proceed into Wednesbury having just traversed the Princes End branch railway.

A view from the top of the gas holder at Tipton gasworks, *c.* 1955. In the street below is a Corporation dust cart, whilst in the far distance is Sedgley Beacon. To the extreme left of the picture are the old Public Offices in Owen Street.

Spring Street off Alexandra Road with the modern gasworks in the background, May 1969.

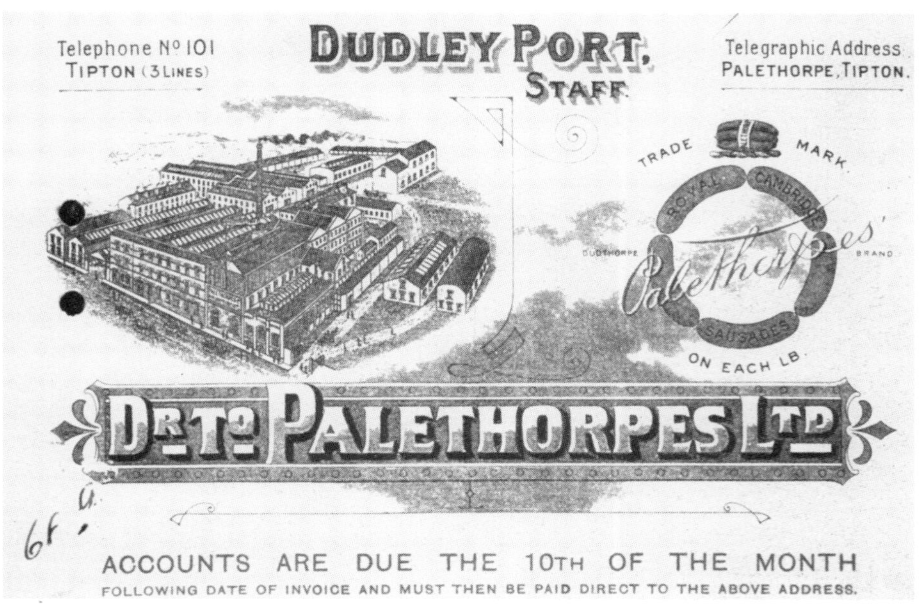

An artist's impression of the extensive sausage making factory owned by Palethorpe's Ltd. at Dudley Port, taken from a company invoice of 1915. This also advertises the well-known brand of sausage the 'Royal Cambridge'.

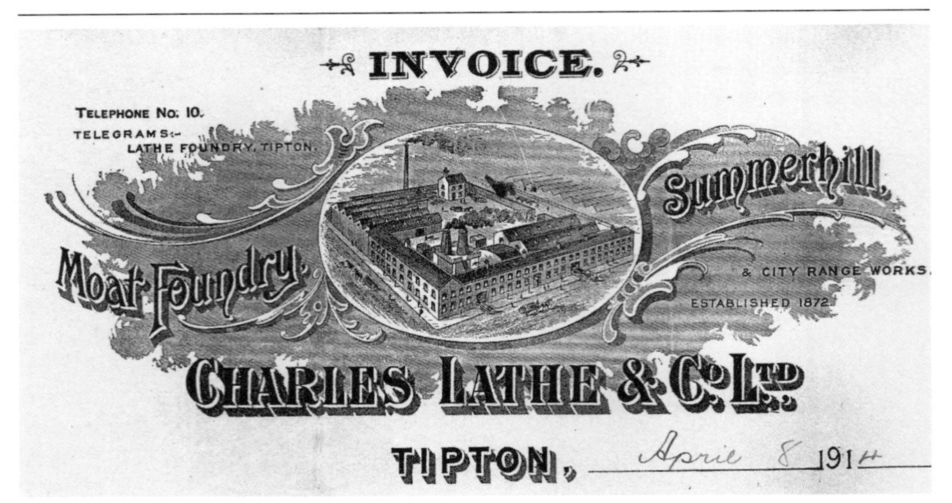
INVOICE.

TELEPHONE No. 10.
TELEGRAMS:-
LATHE FOUNDRY, TIPTON.

Moat Foundry,
Summerhill,
& CITY RANGE WORKS.
ESTABLISHED 1872.

CHARLES LATHE & Co Ltd

TIPTON, April 8 1914

An April 1914 invoice issued by Charles Lathe and Co. Moat Foundry, Summerhill, showing an artist's impression of the works from the air.

A view of the Mond Gas Works, *c.* 1930, with shunting engine *Lance* delivering coke to Hale's Foundry, whose private sidings were accessed through the Gas Works railway system.

Section Ten

CHURCH AND CHAPEL

Choir members of St John's Church, Princes End, late 1920s. The two choristers on the extreme left of the back row were named Callaghan; the priest was Mr Toulouse.

St Martin's Parish Church was erected between 1795 and 1797 to replace the former parish church at Summerhill. Because of the distinctive design of the tower, the church became known as the 'Pepper box'. However, the top of the tower was removed in 1965, along with the peal of eight bells which had been in use since 1848. Inside the church is a memorial to William Rock Small, the former Ringing Master and Tower Keeper, who gave the church over sixty years of service, forty of those as Tower Keeper. The church was declared redundant in the 1980s.

The interior of St Martin's Parish Church, with its distinctly classical style. The stained glass window in the chancel has for its subject the *Good Samaritan*, with the inscription 'To the Glory of God and the adornment of this church, this window was erected by subscription from persons married within its walls, parishioners and other friends. Easter 1878.' The galleries stand on thin iron supports and the organ was erected in 1897.

A rally of the Tipton Union of the Christian Endeavour in 1924, a couple of years after its formation. In the centre of the second row is Ernest Tibbetts, a well-known figure in local Methodist circles.

Park Lane Methodist Church, *c.* 1860. This was the second Methodist chapel to be erected on the Park Lane site, and was enlarged between 1826 and 1827. However, it suffered heavily from mining operations in 1855 and eventually was demolished to make way for the third chapel, which was opened in 1866.

The third Park Lane Methodist Chapel, *c.* 1900. Opened in 1866, it was replaced by a smaller modern building in the 1970s.

Children on the platform during the Tipton Green Methodist Church Sunday School anniversary celebrations, 1951.

St Paul's Methodist Chapel near Dudley Port railway station. Built in 1836, its name was unusual for a nonconformist place of worship in that it contained the name of a saint. This is believed to have derived from early connections with Sir Horace St Paul, a baronet industrialist who had considerable land holdings in Tipton in the mid-nineteenth century.

A Sunday School anniversary procession in Dudley Port, 1920s. In the foreground to the right is the Wrens Nest Inn, one of four public houses in Tipton at that time owned by Wolverhampton and Dudley Breweries. The sign jutting out just beyond shows three horse shoes and probably advertises the smithy of J. Rogers in Sharp Street at the rear of the properties. In the distance is the Old Port bridge crossing the Old Main Line canal.

The Baptist Church, Princes End, Juvenile Concert party, *c.* 1920.

The old cemetery lodge and the entrance to the cemetery, *c.* 1900. The lodge was constructed in a Gothic style in polychrome brick. Along the drive can be seen the spire of the mortuary chapel; this surmounted an archway which divided the chapel into sections for Church of England and Nonconformist mourners. The cemetery was officially opened in March 1873 by Dr McLagan, the then Bishop of Lichfield.

New Road Methodist Church Sunday School anniversary procession, 1953.

A Sunday School canal boat outing for the Toll End Wesleyan Chapel, *c.* 1912.

The members of the Regent Street Methodist Church, *c.* 1920, before the new church was built.

A group of members standing outside Aston Street Methodist Church, Toll End, *c.* 1900.

The rambling Victorian vicarage to St Martin's parish church at No. 1 Dudley Port. The old buildings were demolished in about 1960 and the present vicarage erected in its large walled garden.

Bell Street Methodist Chapel, photographed in 1977 shortly before its closure.

Members of the Horseley Heath Primitive Methodist Church School, 1920. This church was always referred to as the Rhubarb Chapel as rhubarb was once grown in the front garden. The church has a number of subscription bricks built into its fabric.

Section Eleven

ROAD AND RAIL

Owen Street railway crossings and signal box pictured in the early 1960s, when gas lighting was still in use. The line was electrified and the crossing gates replaced with automatic barriers in 1967.

Naylor's garage near The Pound at Toll End, *c.* 1930. The owner, Mr Abraham Naylor, was a one-time member of Tipton Council.

A slightly later view of Naylor's garage, with extended facilities. Brand new Austins and a Morris pose on the forecourt. Note the consecutive registration numbers.

A horse-drawn cart belonging to Palethorpe's Ltd making deliveries in the neighbouring town of Oldbury, *c.* 1900.

A newly built single deck tramcar in the yard of the Tividale tramway workshops, 1917. Situated just outside the Tipton Borough boundary opposite the end of Tividale Street, these works became the central depot for the whole of the Black Country tramway network between 1907 and 1930.

A steam lorry belonging to Wright's Forge and Engineering Co., parked outside the Locomotive Inn, Dudley, *c.* 1928.

A Guy delivery van of 1928 belonging to the Revo Electric Co. Revo was established in 1908 on a canalside site in Tividale and quickly grew to be a major national supplier of electrical street lighting equipment and domestic cookers and fires.

A Clump mooring anchor weighing 8.75 tons made at Neptune Forge being loaded on to a railway wagon at Tipton Goods Yard in the early 1930s.

Ryland Aqueduct, Dudley Port, 1962. A 1952 vintage West Bromwich Corporation bus on the No. 74 service to Dudley has taken necessary advantage of the 15 ft 6 in headroom in the centre lane. The old Dudley Port station can be seen on the railway bridge behind the aqueduct.

A Birmingham Corporation Daimler built in 1948 leaves Tipton and rounds Burnt Tree island *en route* to Dudley, early 1960s. The No. 74 service was operated jointly by Birmingham and West Bromwich Corporations. Note the Borough boundary sign on the left.

A West Bromwich Corporation Daimler bus turns round in Great Bridge, having terminated the No. 76 from Birmingham, 1962. Joseph Wiltshire and Son's pawnbroker's shop can be seen on the right.

A northbound express awaits departure from Dudley Port station in 1961, behind Royal Scot class locomotive No. 46135, the East Lancashire Regiment.

Dudley Port low level station, with a Walsall bound diesel train, August 1963. Passenger services were withdrawn in July 1964 and the attractive blue brick station building demolished in 1967.

A lorry leaving the gates of the Horseley Bridge & Thomas Piggott works, Horseley Road, early 1960s.

A fleet of Hurley's Bakery delivery vans parked outside the bakery in Brown Street, 1959 (prior to being sold to Hickinbottom's).

A lengthy goods train heads for Dudley past Sedgeley Junction signal box, early 1960s. Situated where the railway crossed Sedgley Road East, the box had always had its name mistakenly spelt with an extra 'e' as Sedgeley.

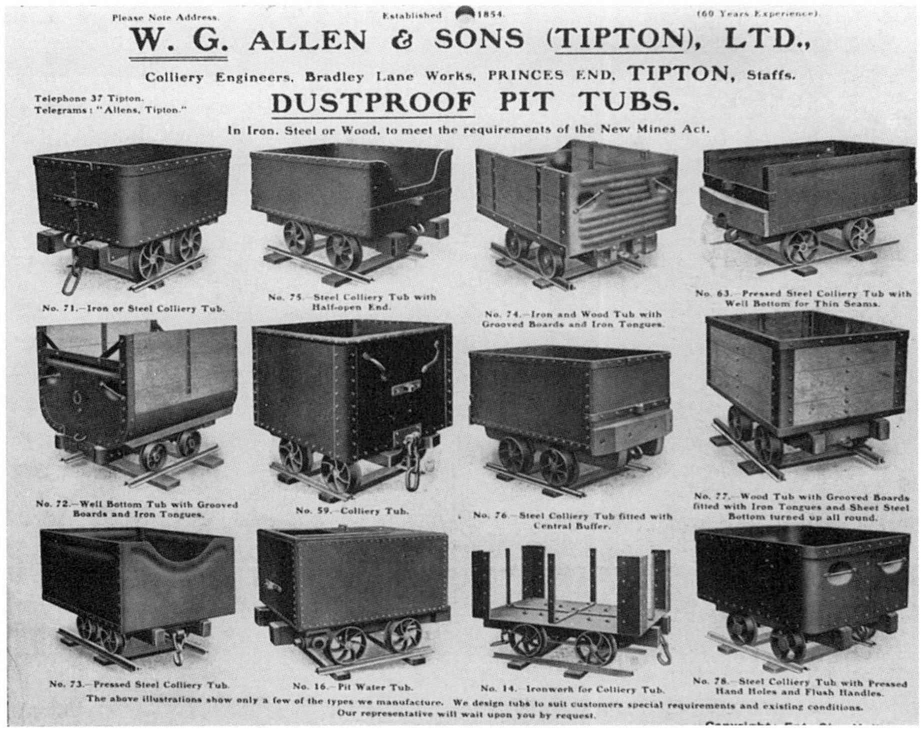

A range of products manufactured by W.G. Allen and Sons illustrating the importance of the coal mining industry locally.

Shunting locomotive J.T. Daly undergoing repair in the works of Horseley Bridge & Thomas Piggot, 1948. The loco was built by Bagnalls of Stafford in 1931 and worked at Tipton until 1969 when it was sold for preservation. In 1982 it was shipped to Alderney in the Channel Islands. J.T. Daly was named after a company chairman of the 1920s.

A Dudley bound goods train blasts through Great Bridge North station, early 1960s.

An open-topped tramcar passes Five Ways and enters Dudley Road on its journey from Wednesbury to Dudley, *c.* 1911. The Darlaston destination is incorrect and suggests a lazy conductor or mischievous children on the top deck.

A British Railways staff bus stands outside the abattoir of W. Devis and Sons Ltd in New Road, Great Bridge, early 1960s. Devis's office building was originally the Bush public house.

A Midland Red Guy bus passes over the level crossing into Owen Street, with the No. 244 service from Wednesbury to Cradley Heath via Great Bridge, 1961.

Percy Guest's garage at Dudley Port, with at least four brands of petrol on sale, 1934. Note the cigarette machine.

A lengthy coal train, banked at the rear, passes through Dudley Port low level station in 1964, a few months after its closure to passenger services. The rebuilding of the high level station had just commenced at that time and the photographer is standing on the temporary footbridge erected to facilitate the reconstruction.

The London Midland and Scottish Railway goods yard at Great Bridge North, *c.* 1930, showing the newly installed 25 ton overhead electric gantry crane.

The Cotterill's Farm dairy cart stands in fields near to the farm, *c.* 1910.

A 1955 Daimler of West Bromwich Corporation stands outside Winroope's chemists in Great Bridge with the No. 74 service to Dudley, 1961.

Section Twelve

SCHOOLDAYS

A classroom at St Martin's School, 1920s. Twins Alf and Fred Perks are amongst the children.

Tipton's first selective higher education schools, the Central Schools, were opened by Councillor Simeon Webb JP, the Chairman of the Tipton Education Committee, on 13 October 1927. The land on which the school was built had been heavily mined for coal and this caused considerable problems during construction. The original schools were divided into sections for boys and girls. In later years the school's status changed to become Tipton Grammar School and later Alexandra High School. The school celebrated its Golden anniversary in 1977 and is still in use in the 1990s.

Some of the girls of Tipton Green Junior School, 1953. The school in Sedgley Road West was built in 1878 and replaced by a new building in Park Lane West in 1976.

Tipton School Boys' Football Club, winners of the H.E. King Cup in 1923–4.

In 1938 Alfred and Fred Perks display the tools and models made by themselves at the Park Lane School's Metalwork Centre during their four years' attendance.

A narrow boat full of school children sets off on a trip from Mitchard's coal wharf along the Old Main Line canal, late 1930s.

The boys of Standard V at Princes End Joint School, *c*. 1925.

A group of young children assemble outside Burnt Tree Board School, *c.* 1895. Situated in Gate Street, the school was opened in 1878 and replaced by a new building in Hill Street, Tividale, in 1967.

Music lessons at Park Lane Infants' School, 1950. The school, actually located in Manor Road, was opened as a temporary building in 1933 and replaced by new facilities in 1995. Tipton Baths can be seen in the background.

Acknowledgements

The authors are pleased to acknowledge the invaluable help which has been given by the following, who have loaned photographs and supplied information:

Mrs E. Arnold • Florence Billingham • Ian Bott • Patricia Bowdler (née Powis)
Alf Breakwell • Ray Brothwood • Andrew Bullock • Chris Burwood • Paul Collins
Trevor and Dorothy Cox • Joshua Churchman • John Deane • Eric Drew
Michael Ellis • Janice Endean • Alan Guest • Gladys Guest • Peter Glews
Mrs I. Griffiths • Michael Hale • Stan Hill • Susan Hill • David Humphries
Gaynor Iddles • Chris Keeling • Ken Kelsey • Jim Lewis • John Maddison
George Marsh • Jean Marsden • Eileen McHugh • Michael Mensing • Margaret Monk
Ike Morgan • George Millward • Ron Moss • Mrs Naylor • Bill Nicholls
John Osborne • Mrs H. Panting • F.J. Parkes • Alf Perks • Fred Perks • Alan Price
Alan Smith • Tony Speak • Jack Stanton • Bill Steventon • Kenneth Tibbetts
Brian Walker • Barry Whitehouse • Harry Whitehouse • Dave Whyley
Margaret Willetts • Ned Williams • David Wilson

Thanks are also due to the following:

Black Country Society • Tipton Civic Society • Sandwell Libraries
Wolverhampton Express and Star • Aerofilms Ltd • British Waterways
Black Country Museum • Boat Museum

Special thanks go to Jonathan Brimble for his help in the production of the book.

THE BLACK COUNTRY SOCIETY

This voluntary society, affiliated to the Civic Trust, was founded in 1967 as a reaction to the trend of the late 1950s and early 1960s to amalgamate everything into large units and in the Midlands to sweep away the area's industrial heritage in the process.

The general aim of the Society is to create interest in the past, present and future of the Black Country, and early on it campaigned for the establishment of an industrial museum. In 1975 the Black Country Museum was started by Dudley Borough Council on 26 acres of totally derelict land adjoining the grounds of Dudley Castle. This has developed into an award-winning museum which attracts over 250,000 visitors annually.

There are over two thousand members of the Black Country Society and all receive the quarterly magazine *The Blackcountryman*, of which over 112 issues have been published since its founding in 1967. In the whole collection there are some 1,700 authoritative articles on all aspects of the Black Country by historians, teachers, researchers, students, subject experts and ordinary folk with an extraordinary story to tell. The whole constitutes a unique resource about the area and is a mine of information for students and researchers who frequently refer to it. Many schools and libraries are subscribers. Three thousand copies of the magazine are printed each quarter. It is non-commercial, and contributors do not receive payment for their articles.

PO Box 71 · Kingswinford · West Midlands DY6 9YN

BRITAIN IN OLD PHOTOGRAPHS

ALDERNEY

Alderney: A Second Selection, *B Bonnard*

BEDFORDSHIRE

Bedfordshire at Work, *N Lutt*

BERKSHIRE

Maidenhead, *M Hayles & D Hedges*
Around Maidenhead, *M Hayles & B Hedges*
Reading, *P Southerton*
Reading: A Second Selection, *P Southerton*
Sandhurst and Crowthorne, *K Dancy*
Around Slough, *J Hunter & K Hunter*
Around Thatcham, *P Allen*
Around Windsor, *B Hedges*

BUCKINGHAMSHIRE

Buckingham and District, *R Cook*
High Wycombe, *R Goodearl*
Around Stony Stratford, *A Lambert*

CHESHIRE

Cheshire Railways, *M Hitches*
Chester, *S Nichols*

CLWYD

Clwyd Railways, *M Hitches*

CLYDESDALE

Clydesdale, *Lesmahagow Parish Historical Association*

CORNWALL

Cornish Coast, *T Bowden*
Falmouth, *P Gilson*
Lower Fal, *P Gilson*
Around Padstow, *M McCarthy*
Around Penzance, *J Holmes*
Penzance and Newlyn, *J Holmes*
Around Truro, *A Lyne*
Upper Fal, *P Gilson*

CUMBERLAND

Cockermouth and District, *J Bernard Bradbury*
Keswick and the Central Lakes, *J Marsh*
Around Penrith, *F Boyd*
Around Whitehaven, *H Fancy*

DERBYSHIRE

Derby, *D Buxton*
Around Matlock, *D Barton*

DEVON

Colyton and Seaton, *T Gosling*
Dawlish and Teignmouth, *G Gosling*
Devon Aerodromes, *K Saunders*
Exeter, *P Thomas*
Exmouth and Budleigh Salterton, *T Gosling*
From Haldon to Mid-Dartmoor, *T Hall*
Honiton and the Otter Valley, *J Yallop*
Around Kingsbridge, *K Tanner*
Around Seaton and Sidmouth, *T Gosling*
Seaton, Axminster and Lyme Regis, *T Gosling*

DORSET

Around Blandford Forum, *B Cox*
Bournemouth, *M Colman*
Bridport and the Bride Valley, *J Burrell & S Humphries*
Dorchester, *T Gosling*
Around Gillingham, *P Crocker*

DURHAM

Darlington, *G Flynn*
Darlington: A Second Selection, *G Flynn*
Durham People, *M Richardson*
Houghton-le-Spring and Hetton-le-Hole, *K Richardson*
Houghton-le-Spring and Hetton-le-Hole: A Second Selection, *K Richardson*
Sunderland, *S Miller & B Bell*
Teesdale, *D Coggins*
Teesdale: A Second Selection, *P Raine*
Weardale, *J Crosby*
Weardale: A Second Selection, *J Crosby*

DYFED

Aberystwyth and North Ceredigion, *Dyfed Cultural Services Dept*
Haverfordwest, *Dyfed Cultural Services Dept*
Upper Tywi Valley, *Dyfed Cultural Services Dept*

ESSEX

Around Grays, *B Evans*

GLOUCESTERSHIRE

Along the Avon from Stratford to Tewkesbury, *J Jeremiah*
Cheltenham: A Second Selection, *R Whiting*
Cheltenham at War, *P Gill*
Cirencester, *J Welsford*
Around Cirencester, *E Cuss & P Griffiths*
Forest, The, *D Mullin*
Gloucester, *J Voyce*
Around Gloucester, *A Sutton*
Gloucester: From the Walwin Collection, *J Voyce*
North Cotswolds, *D Viner*
Severn Vale, *A Sutton*
Stonehouse to Painswick, *A Sutton*
Stroud and the Five Valleys, *S Gardiner & L Padin*
Stroud and the Five Valleys: A Second Selection, *S Gardiner & L Padin*
Stroud's Golden Valley, *S Gardiner & L Padin*
Stroudwater and Thames & Severn Canals, *E Cuss & S Gardiner*
Stroudwater and Thames & Severn Canals: A Second Selection, *E Cuss & S Gardiner*
Tewkesbury and the Vale of Gloucester, *C Hilton*
Thornbury to Berkeley, *J Hudson*
Uley, Dursley and Cam, *A Sutton*
Wotton-under-Edge to Chipping Sodbury, *A Sutton*

GWYNEDD

Anglesey, *M Hitches*
Gwynedd Railways, *M Hitches*
Around Llandudno, *M Hitches*
Vale of Conwy, *M Hitches*

HAMPSHIRE

Gosport, *J Sadden*
Portsmouth, *P Rogers & D Francis*

HEREFORDSHIRE

Herefordshire, *A Sandford*

HERTFORDSHIRE

Barnet, *I Norrie*
Hitchin, *A Fleck*
St Albans, *S Mullins*
Stevenage, *M Appleton*

ISLE OF MAN

The Tourist Trophy, *B Snelling*

ISLE OF WIGHT

Newport, *D Parr*
Around Ryde, *D Parr*

JERSEY

Jersey: A Third Selection, *R Lemprière*

KENT

Bexley, *M Scott*
Broadstairs and St Peter's, *J Whyman*
Bromley, Keston and Hayes, *M Scott*
Canterbury: A Second Selection, *D Butler*
Chatham and Gillingham, *P MacDougall*
Chatham Dockyard, *P MacDougall*
Deal, *J Broady*
Early Broadstairs and St Peter's, *B Wootton*
East Kent at War, *D Collyer*
Eltham, *J Kennett*
Folkestone: A Second Selection, *A Taylor & E Rooney*
Goudhurst to Tenterden, *A Guilmant*
Gravesend, *R Hiscock*
Around Gravesham, *R Hiscock & D Grierson*
Herne Bay, *J Hawkins*
Lympne Airport, *D Collyer*
Maidstone, *I Hales*
Margate, *R Clements*
RAF Hawkinge, *R Humphreys*
RAF Manston, *RAF Manston History Club*
RAF Manston: A Second Selection, *RAF Manston History Club*
Ramsgate and Thanet Life, *D Perkins*
Romney Marsh, *E Carpenter*
Sandwich, *C Wanostrocht*
Around Tonbridge, *C Bell*
Tunbridge Wells, *M Rowlands & I Beavis*
Tunbridge Wells: A Second Selection, *M Rowlands & I Beavis*
Around Whitstable, *C Court*
Wingham, Adisham and Littlebourne, *M Crane*

LANCASHIRE

Around Barrow-in-Furness, *J Garbutt & J Marsh*
Blackpool, *C Rothwell*
Bury, *J Hudson*
Chorley and District, *J Smith*
Fleetwood, *C Rothwell*
Heywood, *J Hudson*
Around Kirkham, *C Rothwell*
Lancashire North of the Sands, *J Garbutt & J Marsh*
Around Lancaster, *S Ashworth*
Lytham St Anne's, *C Rothwell*
North Fylde, *C Rothwell*
Radcliffe, *J Hudson*
Rossendale, *B Moore & N Dunnachie*

LEICESTERSHIRE

Around Ashby-de-la-Zouch, *K Hillier*
Charnwood Forest, *I Keil, W Humphrey & D Wix*
Leicester, *D Burton*
Leicester: A Second Selection, *D Burton*
Melton Mowbray, *T Hickman*
Around Melton Mowbray, *T Hickman*
River Soar, *D Wix, P Shacklock & I Keil*
Rutland, *T Clough*
Vale of Belvoir, *T Hickman*
Around the Welland Valley, *S Mastoris*

LINCOLNSHIRE

Grimsby, *J Tierney*
Around Grimsby, *J Tierney*
Grimsby Docks, *J Tierney*
Lincoln, *D Cuppleditch*

Scunthorpe, *D Taylor*
Skegness, *W Kime*
Around Skegness, *W Kime*

LONDON

Balham and Tooting, *P Loobey*
Crystal Palace, Penge & Anerley, *M Scott*
Greenwich and Woolwich, *K Clark*
Hackney: A Second Selection, *D Mander*
Lewisham and Deptford, *J Coulter*
Lewisham and Deptford: A Second Selection, *J Coulter*
Streatham, *P Loobey*
Around Whetstone and North Finchley, *J Heathfield*
Woolwich, *B Evans*

MONMOUTHSHIRE

Chepstow and the River Wye, *A Rainsbury*
Monmouth and the River Wye, *Monmouth Museum*

NORFOLK

Great Yarmouth, *M Teun*
Norwich, *M Colman*
Wymondham and Attleborough, *P Yaxley*

NORTHAMPTONSHIRE

Around Stony Stratford, *A Lambert*

NOTTINGHAMSHIRE

Arnold and Bestwood, *M Spick*
Arnold and Bestwood: A Second Selection, *M Spick*
Changing Face of Nottingham, *G Oldfield*
Mansfield, *Old Mansfield Society*
Around Newark, *T Warner*
Nottingham: 1944–1974, *D Whitworth*
Sherwood Forest, *D Ottewell*
Victorian Nottingham, *M Payne*

OXFORDSHIRE

Around Abingdon, *P Horn*
Banburyshire, *M Barnett & S Gosling*
Burford, *A Jewell*
Around Didcot and the Hagbournes, *B Lingham*
Garsington, *M Gunther*
Around Henley-on-Thames, *S Ellis*
Oxford: The University, *J Rhodes*
Thame to Watlington, *N Hood*
Around Wallingford, *D Beasley*
Witney, *T Worley*
Around Witney, *C Mitchell*
Witney District, *T Worley*
Around Woodstock, *J Bond*

POWYS

Brecon, *Brecknock Museum*
Welshpool, *E Bredsdorff*

SHROPSHIRE

Shrewsbury, *D Trumper*
Whitchurch to Market Drayton, *M Morris*

SOMERSET

Bath, *J Hudson*
Bridgwater and the River Parrett, *R Fitzhugh*
Bristol, *D Moorcroft & N Campbell-Sharp*
Changing Face of Keynsham, *B Lowe & M Whitehead*
Chard and Ilminster, *G Gosling & F Huddy*
Crewkerne and the Ham Stone Villages, *G Gosling & F Huddy*
Around Keynsham and Saltford, *B Lowe & T Brown*
Midsomer Norton and Radstock, *C Howell*
Somerton, Ilchester and Langport, *G Gosling & F Huddy*
Taunton, *N Chipchase*
Around Taunton, *N Chipchase*
Wells, *C Howell*
Weston-Super-Mare, *S Poole*
Around Weston-Super-Mare, *S Poole*
West Somerset Villages, *K Houghton & L Thomas*

STAFFORDSHIRE

Aldridge, *J Farrow*
Bilston, *E Rees*
Black Country Transport: Aviation, *A Brew*
Around Burton upon Trent, *G Sowerby & R Farman*
Bushbury, *A Chatwin, M Mills & E Rees*
Around Cannock, *M Mills & S Belcher*
Around Leek, *R Poole*
Lichfield, *H Clayton & K Simmons*
Around Pattingham and Wombourne, *M Griffiths, P Leigh & M Mills*
Around Rugeley, *T Randall & J Anslow*
Smethwick, *J Maddison*
Stafford, *J Anslow & T Randall*
Around Stafford, *J Anslow & T Randall*
Stoke-on-Trent, *I Lawley*
Around Tamworth, *R Sulima*
Around Tettenhall and Codsall, *M Mills*
Tipton, Wednesbury and Darlaston, *R Pearson*
Walsall, *D Gilbert & M Lewis*
Wednesbury, *I Bott*
West Bromwich, *R Pearson*

SUFFOLK

Ipswich: A Second Selection, *D Kindred*
Around Ipswich, *D Kindred*
Around Mildenhall, *C Dring*
Southwold to Aldeburgh, *H Phelps*
Around Woodbridge, *H Phelps*

SURREY

Cheam and Belmont, *P Berry*
Croydon, *S Bligh*
Dorking and District, *K Harding*
Around Dorking, *A Jackson*
Around Epsom, *P Berry*
Farnham: A Second Selection, *J Parratt*
Around Haslemere and Hindhead, *T Winter & G Collyer*
Richmond, *Richmond Local History Society*
Sutton, *P Berry*

SUSSEX

Arundel and the Arun Valley, *J Godfrey*
Bishopstone and Seaford, *P Pople & P Berry*
Brighton and Hove, *J Middleton*
Brighton and Hove: A Second Selection, *J Middleton*
Around Crawley, *M Goldsmith*
Hastings, *P Haines*
Hastings: A Second Selection, *P Haines*
Around Haywards Heath, *J Middleton*
Around Heathfield, *A Gillet & B Russell*
Around Heathfield: A Second Selection, *A Gillet & B Russell*
High Weald, *B Harwood*
High Weald: A Second Selection, *B Harwood*
Horsham and District, *T Wales*
Lewes, *J Middleton*
RAF Tangmere, *A Saunders*
Around Rye, *A Dickinson*
Around Worthing, *S White*

WARWICKSHIRE

Along the Avon from Stratford to Tewkesbury, *J Jeremiah*
Bedworth, *J Burton*
Coventry, *D McGrory*
Around Coventry, *D McGrory*
Nuneaton, *S Clews & S Vaughan*
Around Royal Leamington Spa, *J Cameron*
Around Royal Leamington Spa: A Second Selection, *J Cameron*
Around Warwick, *R Booth*

WESTMORLAND

Eden Valley, *J Marsh*
Kendal, *M & P Duff*
South Westmorland Villages, *J Marsh*
Westmorland Lakes, *J Marsh*

WILTSHIRE

Around Amesbury, *P Daniels*
Chippenham and Lacock, *A Wilson & M Wilson*
Around Corsham and Box, *A Wilson & M Wilson*
Around Devizes, *D Buxton*
Around Highworth, *G Tanner*
Around Highworth and Faringdon, *G Tanner*
Around Malmesbury, *A Wilson*
Marlborough: A Second Selection, *P Colman*
Around Melksham, *Melksham and District Historical Association*
Nadder Valley, *R. Sawyer*
Salisbury, *P Saunders*
Salisbury: A Second Selection, *P Daniels*
Salisbury: A Third Selection, *P Daniels*
Around Salisbury, *P Daniels*
Swindon: A Third Selection, *The Swindon Society*
Swindon: A Fourth Selection, *The Swindon Society*
Trowbridge, *M Marshman*
Around Wilton, *P Daniels*
Around Wootton Bassett, Cricklade and Purton, *T Sharp*

WORCESTERSHIRE

Evesham to Bredon, *F Archer*
Around Malvern, *K Smith*
Around Pershore, *M Dowty*
Redditch and the Needle District, *R Saunders*
Redditch: A Second Selection, *R Saunders*
Around Tenbury Wells, *D Green*
Worcester, *M Dowty*
Around Worcester, *R Jones*
Worcester in a Day, *M Dowty*
Worcestershire at Work, *R Jones*

YORKSHIRE

Huddersfield: A Second Selection, *H Wheeler*
Huddersfield: A Third Selection, *H Wheeler*
Leeds Road and Rail, *R Vickers*
Pontefract, *R van Riel*
Scarborough, *D Coggins*
Scarborough's War Years, *R Percy*
Skipton and the Dales, *Friends of the Craven Museum*
Around Skipton-in-Craven, *Friends of the Craven Museum*
Yorkshire Wolds, *I & M Sumner*